AMERICAN TALL TALES
BY
Mary Pope Osborne
WOOD ENGRAVINGS BY
Michael McCurdy

#1 New York Times Bestselling Seri
Night of the Ninth Dragon

the BRAVE LITTLE SEAMSTRESS
Written by
Mary Pope Osborne
Illustrated by
Giselle Potter

CHILDREN'S STORYTELLERS

Mary Pope Osborne

by Chris Bowman

BLASTOFF! READERS

BELLWETHER MEDIA • MINNEAPOLIS, MN

Note to Librarians, Teachers, and Parents:

Blastoff! Readers are carefully developed by literacy experts and combine standards-based content with developmentally appropriate text.

Level 1 provides the most support through repetition of high-frequency words, light text, predictable sentence patterns, and strong visual support.

Level 2 offers early readers a bit more challenge through varied simple sentences, increased text load, and less repetition of high-frequency words.

Level 3 advances early-fluent readers toward fluency through increased text and concept load, less reliance on visuals, longer sentences, and more literary language.

Level 4 builds reading stamina by providing more text per page, increased use of punctuation, greater variation in sentence patterns, and increasingly challenging vocabulary.

Level 5 encourages children to move from "learning to read" to "reading to learn" by providing even more text, varied writing styles, and less familiar topics.

Whichever book is right for your reader, Blastoff! Readers are the perfect books to build confidence and encourage a love of reading that will last a lifetime!

This edition first published in 2018 by Bellwether Media, Inc.

No part of this publication may be reproduced in whole or in part without written permission of the publisher. For information regarding permission, write to Bellwether Media, Inc., Attention: Permissions Department, 5357 Penn Avenue South, Minneapolis, MN 55419.

Library of Congress Cataloging-in-Publication Data

Names: Bowman, Chris, 1990- author.
Title: Mary Pope Osborne / by Chris Bowman.
Description: Minneapolis, MN : Bellwether Media, Inc., 2018. | Series:
   Blastoff! Readers: Children's Storytellers | Includes bibliographical
   references and index. | Audience: Grades 2-5
Identifiers: LCCN 2016055076 (print) | LCCN 2017013274 (ebook) | ISBN
   9781626176492 (hardcover : alk. paper) | ISBN 9781681033792 (ebook)
Subjects: LCSH: Osborne, Mary Pope–Juvenile literature. | Authors,
   American–20th century–Biography–Juvenile literature. | Children's
   stories–Authorship–Juvenile literature.
Classification: LCC PS3565.S443 (ebook) | LCC PS3565.S443 Z55 2018 (print) |
   DDC 813/.54 [B] –dc23
LC record available at https://lccn.loc.gov/2016055076

Editor: Betsy Rathburn   Designer: Josh Brink
Printed in the United States of America, North Mankato, MN.

Table of Contents

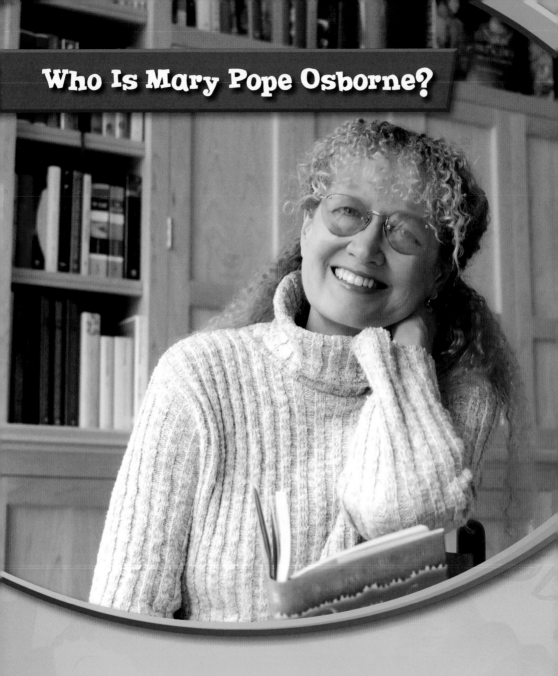

Who Is Mary Pope Osborne?

Mary Pope Osborne is a popular author for children and young adults. She has written over 100 books in her more than 30-year **career**.

Mary's Magic Tree House **series** is a favorite among young readers. More than 130 million copies of these books have been sold worldwide!

"I'm one of those very lucky people who absolutely loves what they do for a living."

Mary Pope Osborne

An Active Imagination

Mary was born on May 20, 1949, in Fort Sill, Oklahoma. She grew up with an older sister, a twin brother, and a younger brother.

Fort Sill, Oklahoma

"I spent all my childhood in a state of make-believe."
Mary Pope Osborne

Mary's father was in the military. This meant the family moved often. They lived in many states, and even in another country.

"Right now, I just want kids to read, read, read."

Mary Pope Osborne

From a young age, Mary had a wild imagination. She often made up stories with her siblings. They pretended that places around military bases were scenes in fairy tales.

Mary's family also loved reading. They often checked out books from the library. They read together every day.

When Mary was a teen, her father retired from the military. But Mary missed traveling. She soon joined a local theater. Now she could have adventures on stage!

After high school, Mary studied drama at the University of North Carolina. She also studied religion. She liked learning about different **cultures** and beliefs.

"When I stepped from the sunny street into that musty-smelling, dark little theater, all things seemed possible."
Mary Pope Osborne

Mary took time to travel after college. She explored many countries in Europe and Asia. She felt like she was living out many of her childhood dreams.

Eventually, Mary moved back to the United States. She worked many different jobs. She spent time as an acting teacher, a waitress, and a **travel agent**.

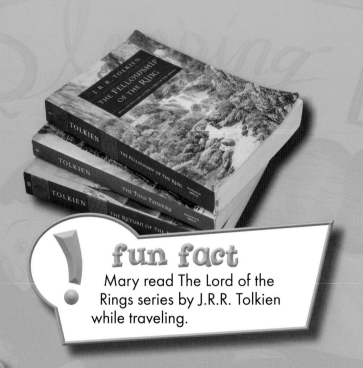

fun fact

Mary read The Lord of the Rings series by J.R.R. Tolkien while traveling.

A Perfect Fit

Mary soon decided to try writing for young readers. Her first book, *Run, Run, as Fast as You Can*, was **published** in 1982. It was about a girl growing up in the South. Mary had found her perfect career!

RUN, RUN, AS FAST AS YOU CAN

Mary Pope Osborne

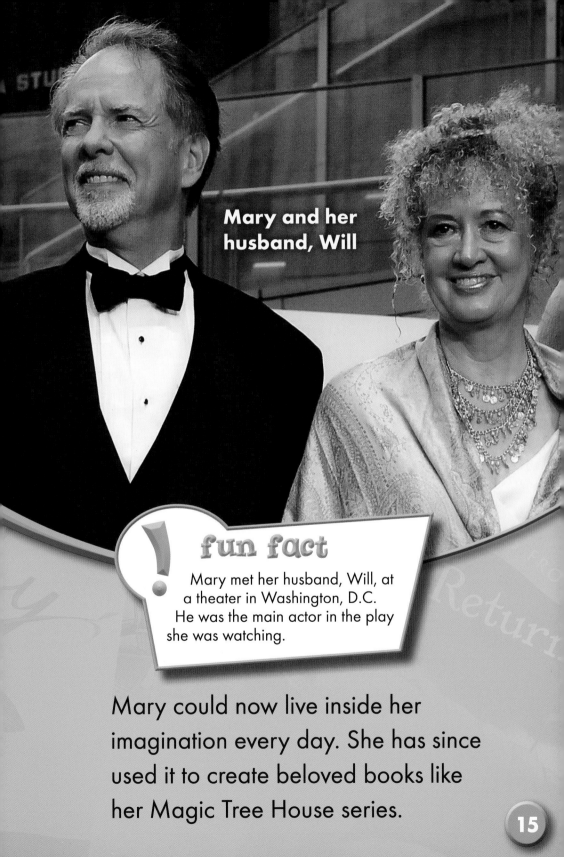

Mary and her husband, Will

fun fact

Mary met her husband, Will, at a theater in Washington, D.C. He was the main actor in the play she was watching.

Mary could now live inside her imagination every day. She has since used it to create beloved books like her Magic Tree House series.

Bringing History to Life

Mary writes for many types of readers. Her books include **novels**, picture books, and mysteries. She also writes **biographies** and new versions of **myths**!

The books usually involve Mary's love of traveling and exploring other cultures. Many of her stories take readers to far-off places and historic times.

SELECTED WORKS

Run, Run, as Fast as You Can (1982)

Favorite Greek Myths (1989)

American Tall Tales (1991)

Magic Tree House series (1992-)

Mermaid Tales From Around the World (1993)

Haunted Waters (1994)

Favorite Norse Myths (1996)

Adaline Falling Star (2000)

Kate and the Beanstalk (2000)

Tales from the Odyssey series (2002-2005)

Mary's books also **inspire** readers to use their creativity while learning. She **encourages** readers to go on adventures with Jack and Annie in the Magic Tree House books.

fun fact

At first, Mary planned the Magic Tree House series to be only four books long. Today, there are over 50!

> "I find that the more you learn, the more you want to learn."
> Mary Pope Osborne

POP CULTURE CONNECTION

Magic Tree House: The Musical combines Mary's love of theater with her books. The show brings the magic of the stories to stages around the country.

Nonfiction books in the series teach readers about topics like history and science. These show the relationship between fact and **fiction**. Mary likes to make learning fun in her books.

Mary's stories delight readers all over the world. Millions of children have fallen in love with reading through her books.

IMPORTANT DATES

1949: Mary is born on May 20 in Fort Sill, Oklahoma.

1982: Mary's first book, *Run, Run, as Fast as You Can*, is published.

1991: *American Tall Tales* receives an ABC Booksellers' Choice Award.

1992: *Dinosaurs Before Dark*, the first Magic Tree House book, comes out.

1994: *Spider Kane and the Mystery at Jumbo Nightcrawler's* is nominated for a Best Juvenile Mystery Edgar Award.

1997: *One World, Many Religions: The Ways We Worship* is named a National Council of Teachers of English Orbis Pictus Honor Book.

2005: Mary receives the Educational Book and Media Association's Jeremiah Ludington Award.

2013: The Magic Tree House series is nominated for a Nickelodeon Kids' Choice Award for Favorite Book.

Mary often gets ideas from her fans. She uses these to plan her next project. Whether they are based on history or myth, Mary's books always take readers on a new adventure!

Glossary

biographies—works that tell the story of a person's life

career—a job someone does for a long time

cultures—the specific beliefs and practices of groups or regions

encourages—gives hope or confidence

fiction—written stories about people and events that are not real

inspire—to give someone an idea about what to do or create

myths—tales of the gods, half-gods, and heroes of a culture or a group of people

nonfiction—writing that is about facts or real events

novels—longer written stories, usually about made-up characters and events

published—printed for a public audience

series—a number of things that are connected in a certain order

travel agent—a person whose job is to arrange transportation, hotels, tours, and trips for travelers

To Learn More

AT THE LIBRARY

Leaf, Christina. *Laura Ingalls Wilder*. Minneapolis, Minn.: Bellwether Media, 2016.

Osborne, Mary Pope. *Dinosaurs Before Dark*. New York, N.Y.: Random House, 1992.

Wheeler, Jill C. *Mary Pope Osborne*. Edina, Minn.: ABDO Pub., 2007.

ON THE WEB

Learning more about Mary Pope Osborne is as easy as 1, 2, 3.

1. Go to www.factsurfer.com.

2. Enter "Mary Pope Osborne" into the search box.

3. Click the "Surf" button and you will see a list of related web sites.

With factsurfer.com, finding more information is just a click away.

Index

The images in this book are reproduced through the courtesy of: PR NEWSWIRE/ AP Images, front cover; Josh Brink, front cover (books), pp. 9, 14, 19; Jessica Hill/ AP Images, pp. 4, 7; Julia Ewan/ Getty Images, p. 5; Kimberly Butler/ Getty Images, p. 8; John Minchillo/ AP Images, pp. 10, 13; Robin Marchant/ Stringer/ Getty Images, pp. 11, 20; Domini Brown, p. 12; Jun Sato/ Getty Images, p. 15; JetBlue and M/ AP Images, p. 16; Christine T. Nguyen/ AP Images, p. 18.

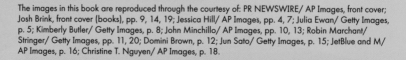